What's It All Worth?

The Value of Money

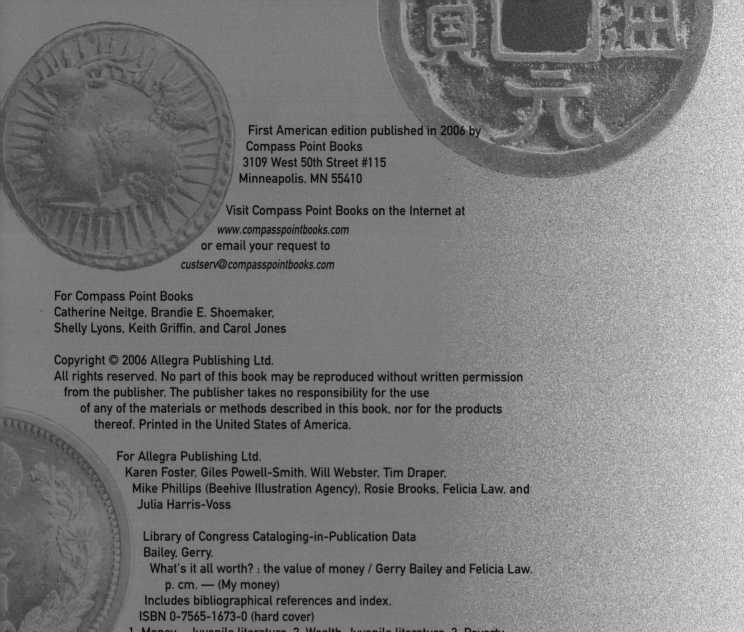

First American edition published in 2006 by
Compass Point Books
3109 West 50th Street #115
Minneapolis, MN 55410

Visit Compass Point Books on the Internet at
www.compasspointbooks.com
or email your request to
custserv@compasspointbooks.com

For Compass Point Books
Catherine Neitge, Brandie E. Shoemaker,
Shelly Lyons, Keith Griffin, and Carol Jones

For Allegra Publishing Ltd.
Karen Foster, Giles Powell-Smith, Will Webster, Tim Draper,
Mike Phillips (Beehive Illustration Agency), Rosie Brooks, Felicia Law, and
Julia Harris-Voss

Library of Congress Cataloging-in-Publication Data
Bailey, Gerry.
  What's it all worth? : the value of money / Gerry Bailey and Felicia Law.
    p. cm. — (My money)
  Includes bibliographical references and index.
  ISBN 0-7565-1673-0 (hard cover)
  1. Money—Juvenile literature. 2. Wealth-Juvenile literature. 3. Poverty—
Juvenile literature. I. Law, Felicia. II. Title. III. Series.
  HG221.5.B257 2006
  339.2'2—dc22   2005030066

The publishers acknowledge the help of Dr. Joseph Santos, associate professor of
economics, South Dakota State University, and Bob Lovitt and Jo Ruff of Greenaway, Chartered
Accountants, Sevenoaks, Kent, UK, for their consultant input.

Photo credit:
AFP/Getty Images: 35

What's It All Worth?

by Gerry Bailey and Felicia Law

Our world is a very divided place in terms of wealth: There are the very rich and the very poor. Half of the world's population—3 billion people—live on less than $2 a day. What's going on?

 COMPASS POINT BOOKS ✦ MINNEAPOLIS, MINNESOTA

The Save the Children foundation helps children from more than 40 countries around the world.

Table of Contents

Rich man, poor man

What does it really mean to be rich or poor? We all think we know. Rich people seem to be able to buy everything they want and poor people can't even buy the things they need. But being labeled rich or poor isn't always that simple. Take this situation for example: A wealthy man lives in a poor country, where he's considered rich compared to everyone else. But if he moved to a rich country, he might be considered poor compared to everyone else. So is he rich? Or is he poor?

You've probably come across the same kind of thing even closer to home. Let's say the guy across from you in math class has a father who drives a BMW and lives in a house in the best part of town. We'd probably consider him rich. And he is, compared to the homeless person you see wheeling a cart through the streets day and night. But if we compared the BMW owner to a billionaire Saudi prince, we'd have to say he was quite poor. So, riches and poverty are relative.

Nevertheless, there are some conditions that everyone would agree represent desperate poverty, and some that amount to fabulous wealth. It's not just individuals that can be rich or poor, either. Countries can also be seen in this way. The United States, for example, is considered to be very rich, while Third World countries, such as the Congo in Africa, are considered poor.

Obviously, money is at the root of poverty, but there are other things that play a part—human nature, luck, geography, and individual skills. Our main interest, though, is money, and how it contributes to being either rich or poor.

A consumer society

How much do you have to have before you're considered to be rich? It depends on the society you live in. We call our society a consumer society. People are often judged in a consumer society by how many possessions they have, the value of those possessions, and the money required to buy them. Those who have the possessions and the money are considered "superior." Those who don't are considered "inferior." But is this really the right way to see things? Perhaps we all put too much emphasis on getting money and showing it off.

The virtue of poverty

So why are things different now? Haven't people always valued riches? Yes, they have. But in times past, only a few people were classed as really rich. Everyone else lived as best they could and placed value on things other than wealth.

In fact, being really poor was considered a virtue for some. Many religions practiced poverty as a virtuous way of life. Learning and religious devotion were highly thought of—NOT possessions.

Two things have happened to change that. First of all, in many countries, science and changing values have led many to question the role of religion in their lives. Many want to live as much as they can for the present. As a result, we tend to see worldly things as more important than spiritual things. Secondly, ordinary people have access to greater wealth than ever before. And that has happened only in the last 50 years or so.

So our values have shifted. Money no longer is considered "the root of all evil." Poverty is seen as the devil in our consumer world. We are either haves or have-nots. But many people believe the emphasis on money has gone too far, and that it's time for a change. Can our money values shift once again? We'll have to wait and see.

Buddhist monks know that true happiness comes when you don't desire to have and control things.

Mahatma Gandhi

Mahatma Gandhi (1869–1948) was an Indian leader who lived at the time when Britain ruled India and Indians were starting to resent this.

Gandhi's great teachings were founded on the belief that everyone should live a simple life. He said we should adopt voluntary simplicity. By this he meant that we should make a decision to live a simple lifestyle, offering our services, being selfless, and emphasizing our responsibilities rather than our rights.

Gandhi led by example—he did his own cooking, wore simple, traditional clothing, spinning the cloth himself. He believed that having possessions, especially property, was a source of inequality that would lead to violence. And he hated violence. "Live simply," he said, "so that others may simply live." He knew the downside of letting money dominate your life.

Rich people

It's often said that "the rich are different." Well, the fact that they may have billions of dollars more than you or I certainly makes them look different. But there's more to it than that. The very rich have probably always been different, and that's why they became so rich in the first place. Perhaps they had a head start. They may have had superior skills in finance or in some particular business or trade.

Some people just seem to have a knack for being in the right place at the right time, or of knowing where to put their money to make it grow. Others are natural leaders who use their personality or power to get people to do things for them, which in turn produces wealth. Still others are born wealthy and privileged. Perhaps another factor is the desire to make money at all costs.

Born rich

Some people are just plain lucky. An accident of birth means they have more money than they'll probably ever need, without having to work for it. Money received in this way is called inherited wealth. We sometimes say it's being "born with a silver spoon in your mouth."

The first super rich

When humans first banded together to form the groups that eventually became societies, they usually had a leader. The leader might have been elected, or chosen by the people, or he or she might have become leader through force of personality or fighting power.

- As societies became larger and more complex, these men or women became the first monarchs and rulers. Because they were able to dominate, those around them often paid some kind of tribute in goods, gold, and labor.
- Another group became prominent when small farms became larger

estates—the landowners. The landowners became rich from the lands they owned. That made them powerful, and they soon formed a second level of power under the rulers.

- A third group of wealthy people emerged when societies began exchanging local produce and goods at their own regional centers and then abroad. They were the merchants.
- A fourth group, the religious leaders, also wielded power and some became very wealthy, although this wasn't always in keeping with their religious beliefs!

As rich as Croesus

Have you ever heard someone say, He or she is "as rich as Croesus!" Well, Croesus was a rich king who, thousands of years ago, reigned over a country called Lydia. He ordered that coins made of pure gold should be stamped with a symbol showing the head of a lion or bull. From then on, coins in many countries were stamped to show their value.

The House of Rothschild

In 1743, a goldsmith named Amschel Moses Bauer opened a counting house in Frankfurt, Germany. Outside the shop he hung a sign picturing an eagle on a red shield. The business was now referred to as the Red (or *Rot*) Shield firm, or in German, the *Rothschild* firm. When Mayer Amschel, his son, took over the business, he changed the family name to Rothschild. And so one of the most famous names in finance was born.

Rothschild's fortunes grew under the leadership of Mayer Amschel. He had learned a great deal about finance and began carefully lending money to individuals. But he soon found that lending to kings and governments was much more profitable! By concentrating on this, his fortune grew. At the same time, he trained his five sons in banking and how to make money, while insisting that the company be kept a family company—so it would be easier to control.

His five sons were sent to different countries in Europe where they soon dominated the banking world. In the 1800s it was said, "There is but one power in Europe and that is Rothschild." This was almost right! By the 19th century, it was reckoned that the Rothschilds controlled half the world's wealth. Today, no one knows how much they control or what their total wealth is —much of it is held under other names.

"If you can actually count your money, then you are not really a rich man."

J. Paul Getty

Rich heads!

The worst that can happen to rich people is not to pay high taxes, but to lose their heads! The French Revolution took place between 1789–1799 and was an uprising by the poor people of France against the power and privileges of the rich. First the king and queen, and then many of the aristocrats, were led to the guillotine and beheaded.

Queen's cash

The British monarchy is a good example of inherited wealth. It comes, not just as cash in the bank, but as lands and other assets that are constantly earning money. The Queen of England's fortune is now estimated at about $660 million. It would be more, except some of the property in her care, like the famous crown jewels guarded in the Tower of London, actually belong to the British people and not to her.

Of course not all inherited wealth comes from being of "noble blood." The Industrial Revolution produced many rich families whose descendants are still benefiting from the family wealth. The children of those who discovered and drilled for oil are doing pretty well. A good modern example of inherited wealth is that of Sam Walton's kids (now grown-ups), who are among the Top 10 richest people in the world. They benefit from the family's Wal-Mart business empire.

Some people don't like the idea of inherited wealth because the benefactor—the person who gets it —doesn't have to do anything or produce anything to benefit. Do you have an opinion on this? In reality, there's little anyone can do to stop rich kids inheriting money as long as they live in a free society. They can be asked to pay very high taxes, though.

Get rich quick

When you watch MTV, or any of the TV programs that show young people making music and becoming famous, you probably think, "Why can't I do that?" After all, some of these stars don't seem to have that much talent! But what's your real motivation? Do you want to make the best music ever? Do you want to become famous for the music you record? Or is it something else? Deep down, what probably motivates many of us is the chance to "get rich quick." And becoming a pop star is one way of doing it. Make a record, sell millions of copies, and become a millionaire overnight.

Sounds good, but the chances of doing it are remote. For every "wanna-be" that makes it in the entertainment world, there are hundreds that flop. The trouble is, we see the successful ones enjoying

their rewards right there in front of us. It may seem as if it's happening all the time and to lots of people, but in reality it isn't. Still, there are ways to get rich quick, such as marrying an heir or heiress, winning the lottery, making a killing on the stock market or, of course, becoming a pop star overnight. And maybe one or two of you might just get lucky one day.

Inherit a fortune

Inheriting isn't always the nicest way to land a windfall (especially if you inherit from a member of your family), but it's often the most unexpected. You almost certainly haven't been waiting for some rich relative to die, and you probably didn't even know they'd mentioned you in their will. As long as the will is legal, your inheritance is yours to do whatever you want with—although depending on what the will states, there may be strings attached: You can't spend it on certain things or until you're a certain age. And be warned—if the inheritance is very big, you may have to pay taxes on it before it's truly yours.

Lottery win

Gambling always involves chance and risk. People win or lose on the toss of a coin or the roll of the dice. Usually we think of gambling as a game of chance, like bingo or roulette. But any time you risk money on a result that'll be decided by a stroke of luck, or on something that's out of your hands, it's a kind of gambling.

Unfortunately, the gambling urge can easily get out of hand and many people become addicted. They can't stop gambling, usually until they've lost everything. So although gambling can be fun, it can also be dangerous. The rule of thumb is people should never gamble more than they can afford to lose.

Marrying for money

You might think marrying for money is a rather immoral way to go about getting rich, but many people do it. Some succeed by chance, while others set out to marry money from the start. They're sometimes called gold diggers. To them, marrying for love is secondary to getting the riches they crave.

As it happens, that's how things used to be. In medieval Europe, for instance, when a man married, he expected a gift from his future wife's family called a dowry. This was usually a sum of money. So the wealthier the bride, the bigger the dowry and the better off you'd be. Today it's frowned upon for men to marry for money, although it's not unheard of. Usually, however, heirs and heiresses tend to marry within their own social circle, keeping the money firmly among the rich.

The 'get rich' pyramid

There are many kinds of money-making scams that'll earn you a small fortune in very little time. Usually an "offer" comes by mail or e-mail.

The scheme might start by suggesting that you pay a small amount, either by mail or through e-mail, to the first person on a list. You then add your own name to the list, move everyone else's name down one and send the letter out to more people. Then you just sit back and wait for someone to send money to you.

Sounds good, but it only works for a few people. Because for everyone on the list who makes money, a far larger number will have to pay out, and at a certain point many will just lose money. No cash is actually being generated here. It's just being moved about. So take a piece of advice, and stay clear of "get rich quick" schemes.

Find buried treasure!

There are plenty of people who dream of finding buried treasure—and who spend much of their time chasing this dream. Armed with metal detectors or old maps, they scour the countryside for buried hoards of coins or valuables from a long gone age. Many follow in the footsteps of the gold rush prospectors, while others hunt nearer to home—in attics and sheds where Granny might have stuffed her diamonds. Others know the value of such things as collectible autographs, stamps, even letters and postcards.

Treasure from the 7th century

In 1938, a guy called Basil Brown got permission to excavate 18 burial mounds in the Suffolk countryside in Britain. Many of the mounds had already been looted, but beneath the largest lay the remains of a 90-foot-long (27 meters) oak ship. And in the ship was a burial chamber containing a sword, a shield, a helmet, jewelry, drinking horns, and silver bowls. No one knows who was buried there, perhaps a king who ruled in the 600s!

Rules of treasure hunting

If you're a dedicated treasure hunter, you'll certainly be hoping for at least one big find. Just imagine coming across a hoard of gold bullion or precious gems, or even a buried chariot. However, before sitting down and counting up the several thousand gold doubloons you've found to see how much you'll be worth, remember that it isn't actually yours!

When treasure is found (mainly gold and silver and valuable coins) it's owned by the government—not by you. Even if it was found on your land or property, it still isn't yours.

But, you'll almost certainly get a reward—and it could be a big one.

Rags to riches

It used to be said of the 1980s that this was the decade of greed. It was about making large amounts of money on the stock exchange. But more importantly, it reflected how making money had become more important than anything else, including caring or being fair in your dealings. These things were simply discarded because they were seen as signs of weakness.

Things have changed since then, but lots of people still want to make money. And there's nothing wrong with this—as long as it's not the only thing you think about. But today, we still love to hear a "rags to riches" story, the tale of a person who rises from poverty to wealth through hard work, inventive thinking, and a dose of good luck.

J.K. Rowling

J.K. Rowling was a single parent with no money to speak of. But she had an idea, and she worked on it until she got it right. She never lost faith in what she was doing. That idea transformed itself into the first Harry Potter book and now, as author J.K. Rowling, she is one of the wealthiest women in the world.

Sarah Breedlove (Madame C.J. Walker)

Sarah Breedlove was born on a Louisiana cotton plantation in 1867. Her parents had been slaves, and she became an orphan at the age of 7. Sarah worked in the cotton fields and in kitchens, but she'd spotted a potential market among black people, and around 1905 began selling hair-care products. She is said to have invented, or perhaps perfected, the hot comb—a device that could be heated and used to manage thick hair. Sarah didn't let her sex or her color or the prejudice against hair straightening get in the way. She continued to produce and sell hair products, going door-to-door herself and using mail order. Her company grew into the Madame C.J. Walker Manufacturing Co., and Sarah became the first self-made female millionaire in the United States.

Aspirations and goals

When you ask children what they want to do when they're older, you often hear the answer, "I want to be famous," or "I want to be rich." But when you ask them how they're going to get there, they usually run out of ideas quite quickly. If your aspiration in life is to become rich, you'd better be ready for a lot of hard work. Becoming wealthy doesn't just happen.

Your first goal should be to study as hard as you possibly can. With money, as well as most things, knowledge is power. And knowledge comes through dedication and hard work.

To make money you have to earn it, so make your education compatible with your goals. Find out which of the jobs that interest you earn the most money, and work toward one of them. You may find that the satisfaction that comes from doing a certain job is worth more than the money it pays. So perhaps the ultimate goal is to find a career that pays very well AND gives you satisfaction.

Use your imagination. You may discover goals other people haven't even thought of. Many people have made money through innovative thinking. But make sure your goals are achievable. Don't set yourself targets that are so high that you have more chance of failure than success. Remember, if you do fall short sometimes, don't give up. Most people who've become really wealthy have had failures. But they've refused to be put off.

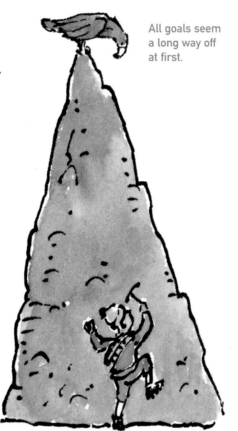

All goals seem a long way off at first.

Horatio Alger

There's a well-known phrase—"It's a true Horatio Alger story." But who was Horatio Alger?

Well, Horatio Alger Jr. was born in Revere, Massachusetts, in 1832, and brought up in a home where education and religion were considered of great importance. After some time in France, he became a minister and social worker. It was during his visits to New York ghettos that he saw the dreadful poverty there.

This inspired him to write the rags-to-riches stories for which he became famous. The theme of his stories was always the same: No matter where you came from, honesty, determination, and hard work would make you a success. He became one of the most popular American writers of the 19th century, with best-selling series such as *Ragged Dick* and *Luck and Pluck*.

Up and down the wealth ladder

Being rich is one thing, staying rich is another. Many people have become rich only to lose it all when fate, greed, or their own poor decision making turned against them. The truly successful ones, though, would have started climbing back up the ladder the next day.

Remember, anything can change, and to lose is not something to be ashamed of. Pick yourself up and start climbing. Failure won't get you sent to the salt mines, so do take risks and try out new ideas—even if the last one didn't work.

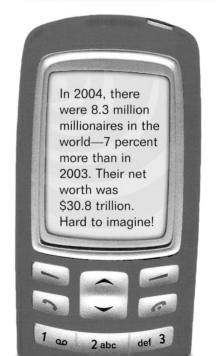

In 2004, there were 8.3 million millionaires in the world—7 percent more than in 2003. Their net worth was $30.8 trillion. Hard to imagine!

Working for wealth

Chances are, that if you're going to make a lot of money, you're going to have to work for it. This generally means entering a profession that pays well, climbing up the corporate ladder of a big company, or becoming an entrepreneur. This is someone who thinks up a project or comes up with a commercial idea. He or she links up his or her enterprise with the two other main factors in business—capital and labor. It's the entrepreneurs, however, who take the risks. They may use their savings to start their business, then organize the labor and capital to continue. They could end up losing everything, or they may become rich beyond their wildest dreams.

The Dyson

The Dyson bagless vacuum cleaner is a good example of an enterprising idea that made James Dyson, the entrepreneur behind it, a fortune. If you've got the self-belief, a great idea, and some money to get started, you might be the next famous entrepreneur. But don't worry if you don't succeed at first. Many wealthy people didn't.

If at first you don't succeed ...

Not everyone gets it right the first time. In fact, you'd be surprised by how many people don't. Here are just a few examples.

David Geffen was a college dropout with apparently no future.

He went on to co-found the Dreamworks film studios now worth more than $3.2 billion.

Marilyn Monroe, famous for her looks, was dropped by Twentieth Century Fox Studios in 1947 because producer Darryl Zanuck thought she was unattractive.

Dr. Seuss's first book, *And to Think that I Saw it on Mulberry Street,* was rejected by 27 publishers and the author even considered burning it.

Peter Benchley, the author of *Jaws,* was fired as a speechwriter for U.S. President Richard Nixon.

John Grisham's book *A Time to Kill* was rejected by 16 agents and 12 publishing houses before it was accepted. He's now one of the world's wealthiest authors.

Walt Disney's first cartoon production company went bankrupt—a good thing for Bambi that he didn't give up.

John F. Kennedy ran for president of his college class and lost.

... try, try, try again

These are just a few of the people who overcame initial setbacks to go on and become famous, wealthy, or both. What they all seemed to show was one of the main ingredients in the entrepreneur's recipe for success: determination.

The recipe for success

When you talk to successful businesspeople, particularly those who've made it as entrepreneurs, they almost always include the same ingredients in their recipe for success. Here are the tastiest:

- Have a clear view of what you want to accomplish, and be focused.
- Believe passionately in yourself and your ability to succeed.
- You can go far if you work hard, are determined, and have foresight, or the ability to predict trends.

- See everything as a positive, even making positives out of negative situations. Learn from mistakes.
- Success can breed success, but don't overreach yourself unless you have a sound business plan.
- Know your business inside out and be hands-on. But be able to delegate to someone in your organization you trust.

- Never rest on your laurels.
- Be opportunistic. Use your hunches and know-how to back a winner.
- Networking: Use the contacts you have to gain knowledge, names, and leads.
- Learn as much about your area of expertise as you can, and prepare a persuasive business plan.

One successful entrepreneur suggested that self-motivation, a bit of brains, some luck, good planning, and effective implementation were the keys to success. Another mentioned absolute self-belief and determination.

When you take on board all of the ingredients mentioned above, these last two seem to sum up the core needs—lots and lots of determination and self-belief. If you possess these, you're off to a good start.

Samuel Slater

When he was a boy, Samuel Slater worked as an apprentice in one of England's textile mills. He wasn't satisfied, however, and wanted to open one of his own in the United States. But he knew that only sheer determination and self-belief would do it for him, since the British had banned the export of textile machines. He got around the ban by committing to memory every detail of the machines' design. He then snuck out of the country disguised as a farm laborer. Nothing was going to stop young Slater, and today he's often referred to as the "Father of American Manufacturers."

Daryl Bernstein

As a kid, Daryl Bernstein owned and ran a number of companies, and in 1992 he published his book *Better Than a Lemonade Stand* to help others become involved in the free enterprise system. He firmly believed that kids could be part of the "business of America that's business" and lost no time in getting involved. His method was to look for needs and charge a fee to fill them, or look for problems and charge a fee for solving them. He believes that business is nothing more than one person trying to make life easier for another. His hobby as a kid was investing his money in the stock market.

Ice-T

Born Tracy Morrow on February 6, 1968, in Newark, New Jersey, Ice-T had a difficult early childhood, to say the least. His parents were killed in a car crash. He then was sent to live with relatives in Los Angeles who didn't take any interest in him at all. Finally, he moved on to a foster home in a very rough area of Los Angeles. His experience and the will to make something of himself prompted him to start rapping in high school. He became so successful, he's often considered to be one of the founding fathers of "gansta" rap. Now he has his own record label, is a movie and television actor, and has written a book, *The Ice Opinion*.

Be a millionaire!

You can be a millionaire! It may take some time, but time is the one thing you've got on your side. Congratulations!

Youth is one of the most priceless commodities in the world, and you've got oodles of it. So plan to use it well.

Slow but sure!

If you put $100 a month into an account that earns about 10 percent per year growth from the time you turn 18, you'll have more than $1 million saved before you turn 65.

Think of every dollar as an employee. Its job is to work for you every day. The money your dollar makes starts to grow in the form of dividends and interest. Start putting your dollars to work. Do you want to spend a dollar on a can of soda that you'll drink in three minutes and never think about again, or do you want to put that dollar to work for you for the rest of your life? OK, right now you're so far away from being 65 that you can't even think about it. But the key to savings is to start now and be consistent. Every month, you should put money into your portfolio and let it go to work for you. On average, your money will double in value every seven years and keep working. If you don't have an account yet, then speak to your parents and go and get one. Start putting a set amount of money in it every month. You're investing in your future and developing the "millionaire" habit. If you put $10 in the bank every month when you're 13, you'll probably be able to put $100 a month in when you're 18, and $1,000 a month in when you're 28.

Where do billionaires live?	
Country	**Number**
1 United States	269
2 Japan	29
3 Germany	28
4 Italy	17
5 Canada	16
6 Switzerland	15
7 France	15
8 Hong Kong	14
9 Mexico	13
10 United Kingdom	12
11 Russia	8
12 Saudi Arabia	8

Millionaires who started small

George Soros

The story of George Soros sums up this spirit. When the Nazis invaded Hungary, the young George Soros was forced to hide, so that he wouldn't be rounded up with his Jewish family and sent to a concentration camp. He had nothing but his wits and a little knowledge of the money markets to help him. Luckily he survived, was able to move to London, and to attend the London School of Economics. He went on to use his knowledge to make billions of dollars. But it wasn't just making money that motivated him. George Soros gives millions to help poorer countries in Eastern Europe. Now a rich man, he doesn't forget his "rags" period.

Tom Monaghan

- Founder
- Company: Domino's Pizza

(Start-up year: 1960)

Tom Monaghan was once a fishmonger. "When I first got out of the orphanage at the age of 12, I'd go out and catch fish on the dock, clean them, and sell them door-to-door."

Charles Schwab

- Chairman
- Company: Charles Schwab

(Start-up year: 1963)

Charles Schwab grew up in a poor family. There was constant talk of not having enough. His first business was raising chickens as a kid. He sold the eggs, the droppings for fertilizer, and, when a chicken got old, he sold the whole thing for the pot. "I sold everything but the feathers."

Misusing wealth

Money should be a force for good. It should make people more content. But we know it doesn't. We know that money, and the lack of it, are the cause of many of the problems in our world today.

Hoarding

Many rich people use their wealth to do work for them. They may travel a lot, or collect works of art, or simply plow it back into the business or venture that made them the money in the first place. Some, however, see the accumulation of money as the only goal worth achieving. They see it as an end to itself, rather than the means to an end. When people hold on to their money for all it's worth, we call them misers, or hoarders.

We usually take a negative view of people who hoard money, and it's not always because we're jealous. From a practical point of view, hoarding money can cause economic problems. The very rich, for instance, can make money without having to do very much at all to earn it. All they need to do is put it in a bank or use some other investment, then sit back and wait for the interest to come rolling in. But if we took that kind of hoarding to its extreme—if all rich people and institutions did that, they'd soon drain all the cash out of the economy, and there'd be none left in circulation for the rest of us to use. So, hoarding isn't a good thing if it's done on a large scale. And it certainly doesn't help the economy to function. It's a misuse of wealth.

Money woes

Money can lead to behavior that causes unhappiness and problems. Here are three examples:

Greed

Greed is a great motivator. It makes people want more than the next person and often forces them to go after things that are way above their ability to achieve. It makes them bend or break laws to get what they want, and it often makes them into bullies.

Once greed takes hold it's difficult to control, especially when you've had a taste of the gains. But, if you're greedy, what you have is never good enough, and so you push for more—until you come crashing down.

The sin of money

As well as being a practical drawback, the hoarding of wealth has been seen by most religions as a very bad thing— even a sin.

Economists also make their point: Hoarding slows or stops the growth of capital. Yet, wealth can be used for the creation of more wealth. If it's left to do nothing, it's bound to reduce the amount of working capital in the economy that could be used for investment in trade, agriculture, and industry. This will slow down the rate of economic development and gradually impoverish the country.

On a large scale, hoarding can cause serious economic damage. It can also cause social damage.

Pride

"Pride comes before a fall," as the saying goes. But surely that's just the crying of someone who's envious or jealous of your accomplishments. There's nothing wrong with being justifiably proud of yourself or your achievements. But where things go wrong is when pride becomes all-consuming; when you allow your pride to blind you to the realities of a situation or when it turns into ugly boastfulness.

Envy

Envy is like jealousy: the green-eyed monster that eats away at people until they can only be happy when the object of their envy is theirs or is destroyed. This sounds a bit heavy, but just look at all the movies and dramas that base their stories on envy or jealousy. It really can be the worm in the apple. We're constantly bombarded with images of people who have things we don't, and who appear to be cooler, more respected, or even better loved. Trying to make people envious is one of the motives of advertising. Why not be content with what you have and strike a blow against envy?

Ebenezer Scrooge

Charles Dickens famously wrote about the misuse of wealth in *A Christmas Carol*.

Ebenezer Scrooge sat at his counting desk. It was Christmas Eve and he would be spending it alone. His partner, Jacob Marley, had died exactly seven years ago to the day, leaving him friendless. But Scrooge didn't care. He hated Christmas!

A knock came at the door. It was Scrooge's nephew Fred, coming to ask him to join his family for Christmas. But Scrooge refused the offer, as he always did. In another part of Scrooge's office, Bob Cratchit, his clerk, warmed himself by a tiny fire. Poorly paid and bullied by Scrooge, he nevertheless had a family Christmas to enjoy.

At the end of the day, Scrooge sat in his empty house and contemplated his meager meal. But as he pondered, he heard a strange sound on the landing, and to his horror, the door opened

and in walked the ghost of his old partner, Jacob Marley! Chains of cash boxes, ledgers, and purses of steel bound the fearful apparition. Marley warned Scrooge that his miserly, grasping ways would lead him to suffer after death, just as Marley was suffering. Scrooge should repent, he said, and listen to the three spirits of Christmas that would shortly visit him.

That night Scrooge awoke to find the spirit of Christmas past. It showed Scrooge his lonely childhood, his loving sister Fran, and finally Belle, the love he gave up in favor of financial gain. A second spirit,

the spirit of Christmas present, showed him the Cratchit family enjoying the Christmas festivity. Finally, the spirit of Christmas future showed Scrooge his own pitiful death. This so frightened him that he vowed to change his ways, and at once took gifts to Bob Cratchit's family and to that of his nephew Fred.

Storing wealth

When we finally achieve our goals and get a mountain of money together, where do we put it? Do we hide it under the mattress or dig a hole and bury it in the ground? These probably aren't the best ways of storing your money.

The simplest answer is to put your cash in a bank, where it will at least be safe. You also have the added benefit of earning interest. Interest is the money a bank pays you in return for being able to invest your money on its own behalf. If your wealth is in things, not cash, you can still be sure the bank will help out. Banks use safes and safety deposit boxes to store their customers' deposits and valuables. And, if you're so wealthy that you own a pile of gold bars, there's even a special bank to help you!

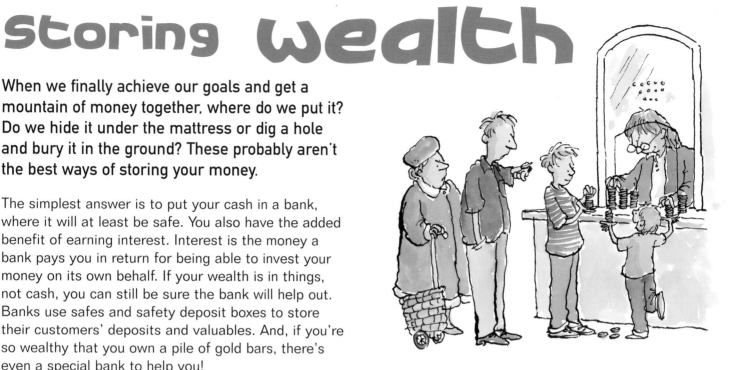

Modern safes

Modern safes generally have two locks. One is operated by a key, while the other is a combination lock, operated by twisting a knob with a pointer that must be turned to a correct combination of numbers. Neither of these locks opens the safe door, however. They release a bolt mechanism that pushes a series of bolts in all directions including the hinge side. So it's no use for a thief trying to chop off the hinges. The doors are thick, with walls of steel and a hollow center filled with concrete.

A safe place

In medieval times, the church used large, beautifully decorated chests as collecting boxes. These chests could be locked securely with a large key to stop people from stealing the contents. In fact, the collection chests were the forerunners of our modern safe. Later on, different kinds of locks were invented and the cabinet, or chest part, was made of strong material such as iron and, later, steel. The name *safe* comes from the use of fireproof cabinets that were built to keep money and important documents safe in case of fire.

Down in the vault

Where do you store gold if you have millions of dollars worth? Well, most large amounts of gold are stored in the vaults of big central banks, such as the Federal Reserve Bank in New York City. The gold that's stored there belongs to the United States and 60 countries and international organizations. In fact, it holds 30 percent of the world's gold reserves, valued at $90 billion.

The gold is held in 122 compartments in the main and auxiliary vaults. The Federal Reserve vault is one of the largest. It rests on the bedrock of Manhattan Island, because this was the only foundation strong enough to support the weight of the vault and the gold inside it. And it's located 100 feet (30 meters) below street level.

The gold is stored in bars shaped a little like bricks, which are taken on pallets by elevator five floors down to the vault. A man in a distant room, who communicates by intercom with the armed guards who guard the gold, operates the elevator. Once inside the vault, the gold is weighed and tested for purity. It's then stored in a compartment secured by a padlock, two combination locks, and a seal.

Hydraulic lifts and belts are used to help lift the gold because of its weight. But moving it around is still heavy work, so stackers work in shifts. They also wear magnesium-covered shoes, in case a bar of gold falls on their feet!

There's no door into the vault. Instead, the entrance is a 10-foot (3-m) passageway cut into a 90-ton (81-metric ton) cylinder of steel. The cylinder revolves in a 140-ton (126-metric ton) steel and concrete frame. The vault is opened or closed by rotating the cylinder 90 degrees in the frame. The gold is kept safe by time and combination locks. But for extra safety, no one person holds all the combinations to the locks.

Tax havens

Not many people like paying taxes. But most people just go on and do it. Some, however, especially those with very large incomes, look for ways to reduce their tax burden. One way of doing this is to put yourself or your money into a tax haven.

A tax haven is a place where certain taxes are raised at a lower rate, or not at all. Different places can be havens for different types of taxes—income, company, etc.—or for different kinds of taxpayers or companies. One way of making use of a tax haven is to move away and live there. Many European athletes, for instance, live in the small European country of Monaco, which has no income tax. If you don't want to move yourself, you can always set up a trust in the tax haven. Any money you then make is technically earned by the trust, and is taxed in the tax haven and not in your own country.

Who's storing what, where?

The largest gold reserves are held by the U.S. Treasury—nearly 262 million ounces (8 million kg) of gold, worth $100 billion.

The biggest gold bar, weighing 440 pounds (200 kg), was made by the Mitsubishi Materials Corporation in December 1999, at the Naoshima Refinery, Kagawa Prefecture, Japan. The gold is 99.99 percent pure. The bar measures 7½ inches (19.5 cm) wide and 16 inches (40.5 cm) long at the base, and is 6½ inches (16 cm) tall. It was put on display for the public in 2000.

Rich countries

As well as rich individuals, there are also rich countries. They usually become wealthy because of the trade they do with other countries, perhaps selling raw materials, such as iron and timber, or even the particular skills of their people.

The richest

The United States is a good example of a country that has vast amounts of raw materials and has used them to become wealthy.

The merchants of the city of Venice in Italy started a powerful trading history hundreds of years ago and became very wealthy. Singapore is a trading hub, but it also creates wealth through its international finance center.

Just as with individuals, money tends to flow toward the richer countries that prosper, and away from poorer countries that do not. Today, most wealthy countries are highly industrial societies and are mostly located in what we call the West, or in the Far East, with Japan and Korea leading the way. Since the early 1900s, industry has been a way to make and increase wealth. Poorer countries are less industrialized and mostly located in Africa and South America.

GDP

The world's richest nations are measured by how much each person living in the country contributes to its overall wealth—or earns—in any year. It's called the gross domestic product or GDP. You can see from the statistics on the next page that there's a huge difference between what the average person in Luxembourg earns per year and the average person in Egypt.

G8

The G8 is a term used to describe the seven wealthiest countries in the world—Canada, France, Italy, Germany, Japan, the United Kingdom, and the United States—plus Russia. The purpose of the G8 is to discuss, and possibly to influence, economic and political situations in the world through an annual summit meeting, as well as various other policy meetings and research gatherings. The location of the summit meeting rotates annually among the member states in the order of France, the United States, the United Kingdom, Russia, Germany, Japan, Italy, and Canada.

Recently, the annual G8 meetings have been the focus of anti-globalization protests. The protesters believe that G8 countries are more interested in increasing their own wealth than in helping poorer countries increase theirs. The protesters believe the poor countries are being exploited by the rich countries.

G8 members in 2005:
- Canada
- France
- Germany
- Italy
- Japan
- Russia
- United Kingdom
- United States

Rich lists

The G8 countries may be the richest industrialized countries in the world, but they aren't necessarily the richest in terms of gross domestic product. Many of the following countries are small, but a high percentage of wealthy people live there—especially countries that have low taxes (tax havens). So here are the richest:

Country	GDP
Richest in Europe & N. America	
Luxembourg	$55,100
Norway	$37,800
United States	$37,800
San Marino	$34,600
Switzerland	$32,700
Denmark	$31,100
Iceland	$30,900
Austria	$30,000
Canada	$29,800
Ireland	$29,600
Belgium	$29,100
United Kingdom	$27,700
France	$27,600
Germany	$27,600
Italy	$26,700
Richest in Africa	
Mauritius	$11,400
South Africa	$10,700
Botswana	$9,000
Seychelles	$7,800
Namibia	$7,200
Richest in Asia	
Japan	$28,200
Singapore	$23,700
Brunei	$18,600
South Korea	$17,800
Palau	$9,000
Malaysia	$9,000
Richest in South America	
Uruguay	$12,800
Argentina	$11,200
Chile	$9,900
Brazil	$7,600
Colombia	$6,300
Richest in Middle East	
UAE	$23,200
Qatar	$21,500
Israel	$19,800
Cyprus	$19,200
Kuwait	$19,000

Country	GDP
Richest in Oceania	
Australia	$29,000
New Zealand	$21,600
Fiji	$5,800
Samoa	$5,600
Naura	$5,000
Richest in Central America	
Costa Rica	$9,100
Panama	$6,300
Belize	$4,900

These numbers, which compare the gross domestic product per capita, tell us how countries compare with one another in terms of individual wealth. You can see that the richest country in Central America is only about a third as rich as France and Germany. This tells us that Central American countries are not as wealthy as European countries. We can also see that small countries in the Middle East are wealthy. Their wealth may have something to do with a valuable natural resource called oil.

Source: Aneki.com

Expensive to live in

Because of their cost of living, some countries are more expensive to live in than others. If you want to make money and live cheaply, these are the places to avoid:

1. Japan
2. South Korea
3. Russia
4. Taiwan
5. Norway
6. Hong Kong
7. Switzerland
8. Denmark
9. Argentina
10. China

But maybe your priorities aren't about money. So here's a small list of the cleanest countries: Finland, Norway, Canada, Sweden, and Switzerland.

Highest-taxed country

Denmark is the country with the highest income tax. In return for the high taxes they pay, citizens of Denmark receive many benefits, including free health care and free higher education.

Poverty

Poverty exists everywhere. Hundreds of millions of people live in poverty, even in the richest nations of the world. It seems incredible that in a world where there's so much wealth and so much money, that anyone should be poor at all. But as yet, our global society has not been able to eliminate poverty. It exists all around us.

We know what we mean when we say a person is wealthy, or rich, even if it is relative. But what do we mean when we say they are poor? Well, it means having little or no wealth, if any at all. However, it also means not being able to contribute to the society in which you live. It means suffering deprivation, illiteracy, and poor health. It means living in areas that take the brunt of environmental damage, such as busy, congested roads, factories, and even waste dumps. And, it means living with little self-respect or hope for the future. More than 1 billion of the world's people live in these conditions.

To make matters worse, the gap between rich and poor is growing. At the end of the last century, the top 20 percent of people living in high-income countries consumed 86 percent of the world's goods and services. The poorest 20 percent consumed just 1.3 percent. Many people think that if we're going to tackle poverty, we have to reduce this gap.

The poverty line

We use a measurement called the poverty line to judge poverty. The poverty line, sometimes called the poverty threshold, is the annual income below which a person cannot afford to buy the basic resources they require in order to live. These resources would include a house to live in, food to eat, fuel for heat, and money for health care. People who have an income below the poverty line are said to have no disposable income. This is a technical phrase that simply means they don't have any money to buy luxury goods. Everything they receive is spent on stuff they absolutely need in order to live.

Given the vast wealth of the United States, you'd think that poverty could not exist here. But in 2004, the poverty rate was 12.7 percent of the population. And things are getting worse. In fact, the number of people in poverty was 37 million, an increase of 1.1 million from 2003.

Child labor

More than 350 million children throughout the world between the ages of 5 and 17 are working. More than 111 million do jobs that are considered dangerous. This means work that could damage their health or affect them mentally as they get older. Ten million are working at some kind of slave labor. Yes, slave labor still exists. And it includes armed conflict, prostitution, and pornography. Just imagine being 6 or 7 years old, working all day in a horrible job, and not being paid for it. These kids are being exploited because they're too poor to do anything about it. Poverty is much more than just being short of money.

Schooling

If the parents of poor children didn't go to school when they were young, chances are their children won't either. This means that poverty can cross generations and cause lower levels of earning potential all around. This isn't only bad for the people involved. It's also bad for the economy of the country they live in. Educating children instead of sending them into the work force will help grow the economy, and so create greater productivity and wealth in future generations.

The Little Match Girl

She held a box of matches in her reddened hands. That day she hadn't sold a single match. If she went home, she'd be beaten. With nowhere to turn, she sat down in a corner between two houses, drew her feet under her, and gazed at the nearby windows, which radiated light and the smell of roast goose.

> I'll light one match to warm myself.

> My grandmother told me that when a star falls a soul goes up to heaven.

When she looked up, she saw bright stars twinkling in the sky. Suddenly one fell to earth.

The author, Hans Christian Andersen, was a master at telling stories with a powerful message. He was writing in the Victorian era, around 1900, when poor people had little chance of receiving help. In fact, the Victorians believed in leaving things as they were— not getting involved with other people's problems. This dramatic and sad story really brought the issue of poverty home to its readers.

The night was bitterly cold. The wind gusted behind the snow, driving it like arrows against the skin. A small girl, a match seller, walked through the wintry streets, bare-headed and barefoot.

While the match burned, it warmed her as if she were sitting in front of a stove. How comfortable she felt! But then the match went out. She struck another and when the light fell on the wall, it revealed the room beyond. A roast goose, stuffed with apples and prunes, steamed and sizzled on a table. She reached for the goose, but as she did so, the match went out.

She decided to light the rest of the matches. In the blaze, her old grandmother stood before her. They embraced in the glow and together they flew up into the heavens, where the child would never feel cold again. In the morning the little match girl was found smiling, with eyes wide open. But her hands, still holding the burned matches, were as cold as ice. She had frozen to death in the night.

She lit another, and found herself sitting under the prettiest Christmas tree she'd ever seen. Thousands of candles burned on its branches. The little girl reached out to touch the candles, but as she did so, the match failed.

Unemployed
or unemployable?
Off to the workhouse

It's an unfortunate fact that many people are poor because they do not, or cannot, work. We call people who don't work unemployed.

In some countries the minimum wage is very low or there's no minimum wage at all. This allows employers to pay a very small wage. Given the choice of working at a boring job for long hours, or doing nothing for just about the same amount of money, some people choose not to work at all.

Unemployment also arises when you lose the job you were in, or cannot find employment that uses the skills you have. Losing a job can be the result of companies moving location or even reducing the workforce. Sometimes the market your company's in just disappears. Whatever the reason, though, unemployment is damaging, not just for the individual but for the economy as a whole. If people are out of work, a country cannot produce as many goods and services and cannot raise as much in taxes.

In days gone by, no one wanted to be out of work. If they found themselves in that position, the consequences could be grim. It might mean starvation, or being sent to the poorhouse or workhouse. Before the Protestant Reformation, people were expected to do certain things, such as feed the poor, visit prisoners, and generally do a few good deeds. But with religious reform, these social obligations fell away. To compensate, laws were made to help out the poor, and these were called poor laws. The Elizabethan poor laws of 1601 created an overseer who supervised poorhouses and almshouses. What kind of pauper, or poor person, someone was determined where they would go.

The poor were divided into groups. Those who would work, but couldn't, were termed deserving poor. Those who could work, but wouldn't, were called idle poor. The deserving poor might be placed in almshouses, where they'd be fed. The idle poor, however, were to be whipped through the streets publicly until they learned the error of their ways, or sent to the poorhouse, or workhouse, to work. The numbers of workhouses grew until, in 1776, there were 2,000 in England, with 20 to 50 inmates in each.

Victorian workhouses had a reputation for being tough places to end up in, but at least they gave the poor a roof overhead and some food.

The Great Depression

The 1920s—the Roaring Twenties—seemed to be one big party. There were dancers known as flappers doing a new dance called the Charleston, pink champagne, and lots more. The Great War—World War I—was over and the future looked bright. Economists, politicians, and businessmen were full of confidence. President Herbert Hoover said the American economy was in a healthy state, and investors were urged to put more money into the stock market. Everyone was investing. Share prices went up and up.

Only a few offered warnings or suggested caution. A New York bank expressed concern that credit rises might go above the rate of business growth. Others saw a danger in the over-investment in stocks. Then economists began to suggest that prosperity was an illusion, that many industries were actually suffering and that even the successful ones weren't doing that well. More importantly, too many people were trying to get rich quick, without putting in any real effort. Politicians continued to predict growing prosperity. It was all businessmen and speculators wanted to hear.

So, in 1928 it seemed that everyone was happy. Then came 1929—and the party was over. On Black Thursday, October 24, the stock market crashed. By November, the value of stocks had decreased by $35 billion. Many investors lost everything, and the crash became one of the causes of the Great Depression that soon followed.

Out of work

During the Great Depression, hundreds of thousands of people lost their jobs. It took 10 years of suffering before confidence was restored and people could find work easily again.

Work to live, live to work

Working at something that has a purpose is an essential human need; in fact, it defines us as human beings. Work is supposed to make us feel that we are contributing, being useful, earning our place on the planet.

Employment, however, has its risks and problems. Some workers are not adequately paid, or work under unsafe conditions. Other people may suffer health issues such as heart disease and stress from working long hours.

Of the 2.2 billion people in the world's labor force, 1.5 billion or so are employed. There are millions of unemployed people, even in the richer countries of North America and Europe. Consequences of unemployment may be deaths, suicides, murders, arrests and imprisonments, abuse, drug addiction, and homelessness. Unemployment is behind the huge problem of world poverty.

Losing it

People love spending money. But some are better at it than others. Very often this is the case when people come into money very quickly, such as after a lottery win. When you've had very little in the past, it's extremely tempting to go on a buying spree and purchase a big house, a couple of luxury cars, and an ocean-going yacht! Sometimes, though, the money runs out much quicker than people realize and they're left with nothing. And sometimes, holding on to your money can cause even greater problems.

Winning Post

In 1988 William Post won $16 million in the Pennsylvania Lottery. He knew that his family would do whatever they could to get their hands on it, though. His younger brother was arrested for hiring a hit man to kill him. Others pestered him until he invested in car and restaurant businesses, from which he received nothing in return. He had to fight lawsuit after lawsuit, including former girlfriends who wanted a share of the winnings. In the end, legal fees and taxes gobbled up what was left, and he now lives on government assistance.

Rags to rags

A New Jersey woman was lucky enough to win two lotteries totaling $5.4 million. But she wasted it all on spending, including gifts and gambling. In fact, in the United States, two out of three lose or spend their winnings within five years. They simply don't plan what to do with it—neither saving it, nor investing it.

Dot-com bubble

Many young people made huge amounts of money very quickly when the dot-com industry first started. But it became a bubble that burst. Many whiz kids lost the millions they made. They spent it lavishly on cars, parties, and homes; but the big mistake was to regard their fortune as real. It was only paper wealth invested in the stocks of one or two companies. If they had bought into more conventional companies, they might have protected their wealth.

Pulling a fast one

Some people lose money because they try to trick the tax authorities. A few get away with it, but not Australian fashion leader Ida Ronen. She owned the family fashion house Dolina, which, along with other enterprises, had earned her a lot of money. Unfortunately, she and her sons failed to declare 90 percent of their takings from the family business to the Australian government. This amounted to $15 million. Now, instead of being a millionaire, she faces up to 20 years in jail.

Falling for it

Some people lose money simply because they're greedy and can't resist an easy fortune if they think there's one to be made. In 1997, a small Canadian mining company called Bre-x convinced investors that they had found the biggest gold mine in the world, somewhere in the vast Indonesian jungle. The find turned out to be a hoax. Needless to say, a number of people lost large sums of money.

Winning games losing money

Sports is big business that pays its top performers big bucks. Some know how to deal with sudden wealth. But others blow it on high living and bad investments.

Losing more than a wife

Many very wealthy people sign what's called a prenuptial agreement before they get married. This limits the amount a husband or wife can get when they divorce. Sometimes, though, it doesn't do much good. When Jack Welch, the retired chairman of General Electric, filed for divorce from Jane Beasley in 2002, he thought his prenup would limit his losses to $15 million —a large enough sum, you might think. However, during the period of their marriage his fortune had grown, and his wife insisted that she'd been partly responsible for that growth. To make matters worse for him, the agreement he thought he could use had expired after 10 years. She got what she wanted—$100 million!

Two Mules

Two mules with heavy packs were strolling along, heading for the big city. One of them carried bags filled with tax money—a real treasure. The other carried sacks of oats.

The mule carrying the oats wore a gilded saddle blanket and fake silver bells around his neck. He walked with his head held proud and high, and wanted everyone to think he was well-off.

His companion, who wore a simple collar, a used blanket, and

faded bags followed, plodding along while minding his own business.

All of a sudden, a band of robbers jumped out from nearby trees and set upon the proud mule carrying the oats. A sword swung, and the bags of grain were slashed open.

Oats flew everywhere. The robbers were so angry they struck at the proud mule, and a large tuft of hair was sliced from his tail.

The robbers vanished, taking no notice of the mule carrying the treasure.

Rich in credit

For better or worse, we live in a society where credit, or borrowing, is a way of life. Borrowing is done in some way by almost everyone, from the worker on a minimum wage to the biggest corporation or country in the world. Everyone is borrowing money.

What is Credit?

Credit is another name for a debt. It's money you borrow and agree to pay back later. Borrowing like this always means getting into debt. The concept of debt used to be frowned upon as morally wrong, but today our societies and economies depend on it to function. We've had to adopt a different attitude. Debt is neither bad nor good. Problems only arise when the borrower cannot pay back the lender.

Any sort of lending is a risk, and today bad debt is dealt with as fairly as it can be. It is not, for instance, a crime. You can't be sent to a debtor's prison, as was once the case. When companies, such as banks or other kinds of businesses, cannot obtain the money owed them, they usually employ someone else to do the chasing. People who do this kind of job are called debt collectors.

Repo man

You often hear people who are in debt saying that they are just waiting to hear the repo man knocking at the door. A repossession agent, or a repo man, works for an agency or on his own. Companies hire him or her to recover merchandise that customers have failed to pay for. The agents don't ask for the merchandise, they simply take it. Repossession agents often encounter dangerous situations because the customers are angry that their merchandise is being taken away.

What is a credit card?

Credit cards first came into use in the 1950s, when organizations such as Diners Club and American Express offered a form of unsecured credit. In other words, it wasn't backed up by any assets or property. These cards evolved from shopper's plates, which were a kind of store card used in the 1920s that could only be used in shops. Store cards, or charge cards, which can be used in a single store or chain only, allowed their customers to buy on credit and pay later.

Debt collecting

Debt collecting has become big business. Banks and finance institutions seldom chase debt for very long. It's easier for them to let someone else do it and allow them to take some of the money owed, or a fee for their work. Creditors also know that a company that depends on collecting debts will be a little more aggressive in trying to get hold of the money.

Of course, debt collectors are sometimes accused of using heavy-handed methods to retrieve money, threatening debtors or trying to scare them into paying up. But on the whole, everyone accepts that most people who get into debt just need time and help to repay their debts.

Islam and usury

The Muslim religion does not view debt in the same way as most other religions. The Islamic economy is concerned with the equal distribution of goods, and does not agree that some people should become rich by lending money to others and by charging interest on the loan. They call this usury, and condemn it as a greedy practice. For Muslims, the person responsible for lending the money must shoulder the debt if the borrower cannot repay it.

All locked up

Imagine being thrown into jail because you couldn't pay your debts! Up until the 19th century, debt was something you avoided if you possibly could. Being in debt was almost the same as being a criminal. In many countries someone who owed money could be sent to jail—to a debtor's prison. Here the debtor languished until all the debts were paid off.

This could be sticky! The debtor couldn't get out of prison until the debts were paid, but equally the debts couldn't be paid until he got out of prison. Luckily for many, someone outside the prison

paid the debts. But if not, the inmates could be stuck there for life.

A better class of debtor

For wealthier debtors, the prisons weren't so bad. In fact, they could be quite enjoyable. In the mid-1800s, Lancaster Castle in England was used as a debtor's prison, and between 300 and 400 debtors were held there at any one time. The governor offered his prisoners the choice of 22 rooms at various prices.

The "rent" provided candles, knives and forks, and the services of a "room-man" who did the cooking, cleaning, and serving. Inmates could buy newspapers, clothing, and food, and have visitors. A market was held in the prison courtyard and they spent a lot of time playing games there.

Redistribution of wealth

We've seen that we live in a world where a few people have a great deal of money and many more can be begging for food. So we'll be looking at some ideas that might help balance things out. But throughout history there have been people who took action to restore the balance, people who believed in taking from the rich and giving to the poor—people like Robin Hood!

Robin Hood was a wonderful archer.

TWANG!

Robin Hood, I claim your land and your home, you are now an outlaw!

The sheriff of Nottingham made Robin Hood an outlaw.

I shall live in Sherwood forest.

We will rob from the rich and give to the poor.

Robin soon found some great friends to help him with his quest.

Much of the "robbing" took place in the forest, which Robin's men knew inside out.

They redistributed the money back to the poor.

Fact or fiction?

Later stories tell how Robin is finally pardoned by King Richard II of England, who returns from fighting overseas and denounces his brother King John, as well as the Sheriff of Nottingham. Robin has his lands returned and becomes Earl of Huntingdon.

No one knows for sure if a real Robin Hood ever existed. But researchers have found evidence of a number of people who could have been the hero on which the legends were based. It's not even certain that Robin's forest was Sherwood. Some investigators believe the legends took place in Barnsdale Forest in Yorkshire and involved different people.

Robin Hood
The legend

Today, Robin Hood would be called a thief or a freedom fighter, depending on your point of view. This would probably be guided by how much money you had in YOUR bank account. And whether Robin Hood had already had a hand in redistributing YOUR wealth to the less well-off.

Songs of old

One thing we should remember is that when the tales of Robin Hood first appeared, most people who enjoyed them couldn't read. So the stories weren't written down, but told in songs, or ballads, by wandering minstrels.

What matters?

In the end, though, it doesn't matter whether Robin Hood really existed or not. His story is what counts, and this has stayed with us for hundreds of years because it illustrates and supports a universal truth. Robin Hood was a fighter against injustice, tyranny, and the hoarding of wealth by a privileged few. He was a supporter of the poor and the oppressed.

Poor countries

Just like people, whole countries can be considered poor. A poor country is one that has a low gross domestic product (GDP) per person, one that has few natural resources, or one that doesn't export many goods to make money. The reasons behind the poverty can be put down to natural causes such as the weather, soil makeup, or geography. It's difficult to grow enough to feed the population or sell abroad if the land is desert. Or perhaps there aren't any rich minerals or metals or oil to be mined and sold. After all, some of the richest countries in the world are desertlands—but they do have oil to drill and sell. Many factors may contribute to making a country poor.

Here is a list of the world's 12 poorest countries by GDP per capita in U.S. dollars:

Country	GDP
East Timor	$500
Sierra Leone	$500
Somalia	$500
Burundi	$600
Malawi	$600
Tanzania	$600
Afghanistan	$700
Comoros	$700
Congo, Dem. Rep.	$700
Congo, Republic of	$700
Eritrea	$700
Ethiopia	$700

Don't forget that these are average amounts. This means that although some may earn more, many will earn far less than the average GDP in a year. Notice also how many of the world's poorest countries are in Africa. In fact, the World Bank estimated that three quarters of the poorest, most indebted countries are in Africa.

Why poor?

There are many reasons why some countries are poor. Climate may play a part. If, for instance, a country such as Ethiopia is dependent on farming and there are fierce droughts, many people will suffer—even to the point of starvation. Often, the prevailing climate conditions and unexpected natural disasters contribute to poverty.

No resources

There may be few natural resources a country can use to either develop its own economy or to sell abroad as exports. Or, it may not have easy access to foreign markets. In many poor countries there's no history of modern industry, which has created wealth for the industrialized countries of the world. Also, some of the poor countries have been dependent on commodities that have dropped in value.

War

One of the worst disasters has happened since the country of Ethiopia went to war with its neighbor Eritrea in 1998. Millions of dollars were spent on soldiers and military equipment that could have been used to buy food. It is estimated that $1 million a day was being spent on the war, as well as $80 million each on jet attacks. One thing that has contributed hugely to the plight of poor countries, and continues to do so, is debt. Many of the poor countries have borrowed money from rich countries over the years to help feed their people—even to help pay for their wars.

Disasters

A terrible drought

Unfortunately, no one can do much about a natural disaster until after it's happened. Or can they? Could the drought-initiated famine in Ethiopia in 2000 have been prevented? Probably not, is the answer. The Horn of Africa has a history of drought. The only difference is that droughts are now happening every five years instead of every 10 to 15 years, and they are more severe than ever.

Other factors contributed to the famine as well, including a high population growth rate, smaller farm sizes, poor farming techniques, deforestation, and degraded soil. Each year, 2 billion tons (1.8 billion metric tons) of topsoil is either blown away or washed down the Blue Nile to Egypt. About 80 percent of the population in Ethiopia depends on rain and good topsoil to support its farming. Another factor is the switch to cattle rearing instead of camel rearing. Cattle are more profitable in the short term, but they cannot withstand drought as camels can. Given the size of the problem, it's easy to see why a natural disaster such as drought can cause terrible suffering. Band Aid showed the problem to the world in 1984 and 1985, but Ethiopia still depends on food aid to feed millions of its people.

Global warming

When we pour tons and tons of pollution into the atmosphere it has disastrous consequences. The atmosphere becomes more difficult to breathe, plants are killed, and whole ecosystems can be altered. At the root of it all, the protective atmosphere that surrounds Earth is breaking down because of the presence of gases like carbon dioxide, nitrous oxide, and methane. The sun's rays are penetrating the atmosphere more and more each year—and warming up our climate.

Kyoto Summit

There is new and stronger evidence that most of the warming observed over the past 50 years is attributable to human activities. The telltale signs are melting glaciers, rising seas, droughts, and wild fires. It's estimated that the overall world temperature has gone up 1 degree Fahrenheit and that if nothing is done, the likelihood is that it will increase by between 2.5 degrees and 10.4 degrees in the next 100 years. The results will change our planet!

Given these forecasts, many governments met at Kyoto in Japan in 1997 to decide what should be done. Some countries opposed the idea of reducing energy and argued that global warming might not happen anyway. In the end, 35 nations agreed to cut emissions by an average of 5 percent below the 1990 level by 2012. The United States, the largest user of energy in the world, and Australia did not sign. Any damage caused by global warming will affect poor countries more than wealthy ones, which have the resources to deal with it.

Third World debt

We all know what it means to have a personal debt we can't repay—even if it's just to our mom! But what if it's a country that's borrowed the money and can't pay back the debt? In 2000, the World Bank classified 42 countries as being in debt. These countries are sometimes called HIPCs, which means "heavily indebted poor countries." Many now have debts so great that they cannot pay all the interest on them—let alone pay back the debt itself. And to make matters worse, debt repayment is using up the money that could be better spent on health, education, and building. But things are about to change!

The cost of borrowing

Most of the problems with debt began in the 1970s and 1980s. During those years, many poor countries borrowed money to fund local projects on the back of a price boom. Commodities such as coffee, tea, and metals were fetching high prices, and countries that were rich in commodities bet that the prices would remain high. High prices would, in turn, increase export earnings. The commodities boom also took in the lenders. All they could see were huge profits from their loans. Few took into account what might happen if prices dropped. And drop they did!

The shocking rise in oil prices at the time was partly to blame. It caused a recession worldwide. Interest rates rose and commodity prices fell. Some countries were able to climb out of the difficult times, but others weren't. The debts of struggling countries were now too great to pay. Lenders had to rewrite the loans to make the repayments easier. This gave a country a longer time to pay back, but it didn't reduce the debt. Something more drastic had to be done.

Payback time!

The money borrowed by poorer countries to help feed their people, and even to help pay for their wars, has been costing them heavily in interest. Some pay $13 in repayment for every $1 borrowed!

Now, at last, there are moves to cancel these debts once and for all. Many people believe that poor countries need to get rid of their debt burdens and that these should simply be written off and forgotten.

Foreign investors report:

- Ten percent of sales in Eritrea, India, and Kenya is used to pay for the upkeep of the electric power supply that keeps going on and off.

- Six percent of sales pays for bribes in Armenia, Cambodia, and Nicaragua.

Make poverty history!

The campaign to reduce world poverty once and for all came to a head in July 2005, when people from all over the world gathered in 10 cities to protest. Their placards and banners said it all: "Make poverty history!" For years, we've seen images of dreadful poverty, especially in Africa, and now everyone wanted action. So, people came together at concerts and on marches, and it seemed as if the world's leaders were listening.

Debt Relief Now

$70 a year

That's how much it would cost in aid, per African, to change the continent in this century. What would it accomplish? Both malaria, the disease carried by mosquitoes, and the AIDS virus are huge killers in Africa. Aid would make drugs, immunization, and medical care available to everyone. In seven countries of Africa, people can only expect to live to the age of 40 or less. Compare that to our life expectancy of nearly 78 years!

Trade restrictions would be lifted to help local farmers, and new roads would be built to move their produce to market. People in the countryside would be wealthier and better fed as a result.

In Eritrea, 71 percent of the population doesn't have enough food to grow and stay healthy. In addition, schools would be built and education would be free.

The next generation would be better educated and able to help in the community.

Fair trade

For many years, help from richer countries has come at a price. Many of the rich countries produce more food than they need. But rather than tell their farmers to produce less, they've insisted that the poorer countries take their surplus mountains of sugar, wheat, rice, and so on, at bargain prices. In fact, the imported food ended up being cheaper to buy than local produce. So while the farmers in the rich countries were OK, the farmers in the poor countries suffered. Many people want this arrangement to stop.

Think as you drink

The next time your parents order a cup of coffee, think about where the coffee beans came from that were ground up to make their drink. Chances are they came from a country where the price of beans has dropped over the past few years. You might notice, by the way, that the price of their expensive cup of latte has not. This price drop has hit some coffee growers hard, especially in Ethiopia, where the drought has reduced the quality of the beans. So, while coffee companies make large profits and consumers spend millions at their outlets, coffee farmers have been reduced to poverty.

Some changes are being made. Fair Trade coffee offers farmers a fair price for their beans, and many outlets now serve it or sell it.

Charities

Charities are organizations that offer help in many different forms to those in need. There are many well-known charities that you will have heard of—and maybe helped from time to time. They have an excellent reputation for rushing to a disaster area and bringing immediate relief.

UNICEF

The United Nations Children's Fund, or UNICEF, is a charity that works for children's rights, their survival, their development, and their protection. This involves projects such as providing a good basic education, especially for girls who live in countries where education for them is often denied. Health projects are also important. UNICEF tries to reach as many children as possible with life-saving vaccines. Exploited or abused children are a priority. Many children are forced into the army or into sweatshops where they work long hours for little pay. UNICEF works with civic groups to help create a protective environment for these children. Very young children are not forgotten, and it is UNICEF's aim to see that every newborn child gets the best possible start in life.

Red Cross

The Red Cross and Red Crescent Movement is the largest independent humanitarian network in the world, with more than 100 million members. A Swiss businessman named Henry Dunant began the Red Cross in 1863 after he'd seen the terrible state of soldiers after the battle of Solferino. His dream has turned into an organization that aims to provide a rapid response to disasters and conflicts around the world. It offers food, water, shelter, and medical supplies, as well as provides training and repairs hospitals. It also advises countries, impartially, on global issues such as women's rights and war and land mine awareness. At present, the movement is considering using a third emblem, the red crystal, because the existing ones have religious connections. But the work of the charity will remain the same.

Oxfam

According to the charity Oxfam, the lives of all human beings are of equal value. With this in mind, Oxfam works to overcome suffering and poverty throughout the world. Poverty, in particular, it believes, is an injustice in a world full of resources and is made worse by unequal power among people and nations.

It sees one of its aims, therefore, as helping to change unjust policies and practices.

Oxfam began in 1942 as the Oxford Committee for Famine Relief, helping famine-stricken Greeks during World War II. In 1949 it broadened its goals to the relief of suffering arising from wars and other causes in all parts of the world. Oxfam became its legal name in 1965.

As well as working for the poor, it set up Make Trade Fair, which helps farmers and traders in developing countries get a fair price for their goods.

Save the Children

Save the Children was founded in the United States in 1932 as a charitable child-help program. Today it works in 40 countries around the world. Its aim is to help families improve the health and educational opportunities of their children, as well as to provide money where needed. It is able to mobilize rapid life-support assistance for children caught in natural disasters, such as the tsunami that hit South Asia on December 26, 2004, and man-made ones, such as wars. The charity distributes basic staples such as rice, milk, and bread in places like the Sudan, where drought conditions have been made worse by poor health practices that cause malnutrition and other diseases.

Within two months of the tsunami, world donations topped $526 million.

World Wildlife Fund

Everyone recognizes the great panda logo of the World Wildlife Fund, or WWF. But how many people know that the panda is an endangered species? It's part of the job of the WWF to make this known. For more than 40 years, the WWF has led international efforts to protect endangered species and their habitats. It works in 100 different countries and has 5 million members worldwide. As well as protecting wildlife, the WWF is involved in solving issues such as toxin pollution, over-fishing, and climate change. It advocates the conservation of nature, both animals and plants, and fights for the use of renewable natural resources and the more efficient use of the resources we already use. You can help the WWF by adopting a polar bear or snow leopard.

Amnesty International

When two Portuguese students raised a toast to freedom more than 40 years ago in a Lisbon bar, they were jailed for seven years. British lawyer Peter Berenson felt that this was a terrible act against basic human rights and campaigned to have them freed. He wrote to newspapers and had protests sent to authorities around the world to appeal on behalf of the "forgotten prisoners." This was the beginning of Amnesty International, a movement of people who campaign for internationally recognized human rights. Their guide is the Universal Declaration of Human Rights and other human rights standards. Amnesty researches and takes action to prevent abuses of people's basic human rights both physical and mental, their freedom of conscience and expression, and their freedom from discrimination. The movement won the Nobel Peace Prize in 1977.

Fund-raising ideas

You can do your part to raise money for charity.

Sport:
coaching little kids
golf caddie

Odd jobs:
garage cleaning
spring cleaning
washing windows
painting
trash collection
gardening
car wash

Family:
babysitting
adopt a grandparent
plant sitting
birthday parties
cleaning

Animals:
pet walking
horse grooming

Sales:
used books
plants
wild fruits
household stuff

Deliveries:
paper route
fliers

Entertainment:
party tricks

Make and do:
Easter baskets
T-shirts
sweets, candy, cookies
tree decorations
greeting cards

Rich and happy?

Most of us aren't millionaires. We probably never will be or even want to be. Many of us aren't terribly poor. Most of us are somewhere in the middle—sheltered, fed, clothed, and educated. Above all, most of us live in families that love us and have friends to keep us company. And most of us are happy to be where we are. Or nearly! It's difficult to live in our modern world and not want just those few extra things that the ads say you absolutely need. But then, we know if we work a little harder and a little longer, we might just be able to save up for them. So wanting something often gives us a kick-start and releases new energy—it doesn't make us horribly miserable.

The kingdom of Bhutan

In the kingdom of Bhutan, a mountainous country high in the Himalayan mountains, King Jigme Singye Wangchuck also believes that happiness is more important than wealth. Bhutan is the only country in the world to measure its well-being by gross national happiness (GNH). Most countries worry about their ability to buy and sell the things they make and whether they can afford all the things they need and want. But not Bhutan!

King Wangchuck thinks that if his country tries to develop in line with other countries, it will need to sacrifice its old-fashioned traditions, its heritage and culture, and its beautiful mountain environment.

Gross National Happiness

The Bhutan Parliament made GNH an official policy. Bhutan limits the number of tourists, for example, because its citizens were worried that the environment was being affected and sacred lands were being spoiled. Wealth and progress aren't banned, but they must not hurt the value of human life or people's spiritual well being. Happiness is more important than monetary wealth.

You decide

Our response to money determines what kind of person we are. Look at the topics in this box and decide which of the three options would best match your approach. Then add up whether you have more "a" answers, "b" answers, or "c" answers.

Time and money

a. Work to live, and live for today, for tomorrow is another day.
b. Work, work, work, because time is money. Leisure comes later.
c. Organize your life so you can find time for both work and play.

All about money?

So is Bhutan right? Should the success of a nation be judged by its ability to produce and consume, or should it be based on the quality of life in that country, the happiness of its people?

Should we put more value on things such as fresh water, green forests, clean air, traditional ways of life? If a country makes money from cutting down trees, should it not deduct the loss of the forest from its profits? In many societies, people work at unpaid jobs caring for others, but few countries put a value on their contribution. In Buddhism, happiness is not determined by what we have and own (although this can be useful in reducing poverty and allowing generosity), but by our knowledge, our imagination, and our living skills. What do you think?

Midas

Money and happiness

a. Money can't buy happiness but it sure can buy a lot of fun.

b. Money equals power; power equals happiness; therefore money equals happiness.

c. Money buys respect and status.

How much is enough?

a. Enough to springboard and try more money-making possibilities.

b. 20 percent more than I make now.

c. Enough to guarantee comfort and peace of mind.

Your answers:

a. If most of your answers are "a" you are very relaxed when it comes to cash.

b. If most of your answers are "b" you are driving for success and money.

c. If most of your answers are "c" you have a balance.

The Greek legend of King Midas tells how the lucky monarch was granted his dearest wish by the god of wine, Bacchus.

Midas was greedy, though, and wished that everything he touched would turn to gold. His wish came true. And while he strolled through the palace gardens, to his delight, as his fingers brushed lightly against them, the branches, leaves, and flowers within turned to gold. Overjoyed with his good fortune, King Midas invited all his friends to a great feast. He couldn't wait to demonstrate his new gift to everyone.

All eyes turned on Midas as he raised his glass to toast Bacchus. But, to his horror, the wine poured out as gold dust. Midas gasped and wildly seized bits of food, but each handful turned instantly to gold.

Terrified that he would starve to death, Midas begged to be freed from his wish. Bacchus ordered him to bathe in a magic river, and his golden touch was washed away.

From then on, King Midas lived a simple life and hated gold.

The World Bank normally measures monetary wealth when it looks at the progress in its 180 member countries around the world. But now its Wealth Index measures things like educational offerings, human rights, and life-expectancy, as well as cultural values and activities.

So when you're trying to decide if you belong in the rich or poor league, think outside the dollars. Perhaps you're rich in friends, rich in musical talent, rich in good looks or a great personality, or in supportive parents. Maybe the wealth of opportunities you can tap into in your life are more valuable than money in the bank.

Glossary

accountant

An accountant is a person who prepares the record of financial transactions of a business or individual.

apprentice

An apprentice is someone who works with an expert to learn his or her trade.

asset

An asset is any form of possession that has value.

billionaire

A billionaire is a person who has a billion units of currency.

Buddhism

Buddhism is one of the great religions of the world. It is practiced in many countries of Asia.

bullion

Bullion is gold or silver before it is made into coins.

business plan

A business plan is a document that sets out the future activities and goals of a company.

capital

The capital of a business is the amount of money invested in it.

commodity

A commodity is goods like grain, gold, or oil, that is traded in the belief that it will be worth more later so it can be sold for a profit.

consumer

A consumer is someone who buys things for their own use.

copyright

Copyright is a law that protects the ownership of a work.

credit

Credit is an arrangement a customer can make to pay for goods at a later date.

debt

A debt is an amount of money that is owed to someone.

debtor's prison

In the past, a person in debt could be imprisoned in a debtor's prison until the debts were repaid.

Depression

The Great Depression was a time in the 1930s when the economy was not very active and many people became unemployed. Factories made fewer products and people bought fewer goods.

dividend

A dividend is money paid by a company to its shareholders.

dollar

The dollar is the unit of currency used by many countries of the world, including Australia, Canada, Hong Kong, Taiwan, and the United States.

doubloon

A doubloon was a gold coin that was used in Spain until the 1800s.

dowry

A dowry is money and goods taken by a bride to the family of the bridegroom.

economics

Economics is the study of all the ways in which goods and services are produced, distributed, and used.

economy

The economy of a country is everything to do with the way it produces things and sells them.

ecosystem

An ecosystem is the name given to a community of plants and animals that live and depend upon each other.

entrepreneur

An entrepreneur is a businessperson who organizes, manages, and assumes the risks of a business.

environment

An environment is another name for surroundings that have special conditions and characteristics.

export

To export means to sell goods or services to customers in other countries.

Fair Trade

Fair Trade is the name given to a movement that wants to see certain international trade laws changed.

Federal Reserve Bank
The Federal Reserve is the central bank of the United States.

G8
The G8 is the name given to a group of eight countries representing some of the most industrial and wealthiest in the world.

gamble
To gamble means to take a risk to make money.

GDP
Gross domestic product (GDP) is a measure of how much each individual in a country contributes to the wealth of that country by their labor. GDP is also a measure of the average national wage-earning level.

GNH
GNH stands for gross national happiness and is a measure of how happy the people living in a country are.

gold reserve
Gold reserves are stores of gold, usually owned by governments, which are stored in special vaults.

Gold Rush
The Gold Rush took place in California in the 1840s and 1850s. Hundreds of thousands of people rushed to look for gold in the rivers there.

HIPC
HIPC stands for Heavily Indebted Poor Countries. These are nations that have borrowed money from wealthier nations and are struggling to repay the loans.

inheritance
An inheritance is an amount of money or goods received as a gift on someone's death.

interest
Interest is the price a lender charges to someone who is borrowing money. It is a percentage of the value of the loan.

invest
To invest means to spend money in order to earn more money.

loan
A loan is an amount of money that someone borrows. Interest is usually charged on a loan.

lottery
A lottery is a way of raising money by selling numbered tickets. The winning ticket holder wins a prize.

magnesium
Magnesium is an element found in many minerals and in seawater.

mail order
Mail order is a way of buying goods without having to go to a store. A mail order company advertises its goods in a catalog or online, and the goods are then supplied by mail to the customer.

millionaire
A millionaire is someone who has a million units of currency.

minimum wage
The minimum wage is a standard level of money set by a government as the lowest legal wage that can be paid to someone.

miser
A miser is a person who saves money and will not spend it.

natural resource
A natural resource is any useful substance found on our planet. Forests are a natural resource.

pollution
Pollution describes any form of damage that is done to the environment of Earth and its surrounding atmosphere.

portfolio
A portfolio is a list of investments owned by a company or an individual.

profit
Profit is the money earned when income is greater than expenditure.

real estate

Real estate is a term that means buildings and the land they are built on.

recession

Recession is the name given to a period of time in which businesses reduce their activity.

redistribution of wealth

The redistribution of wealth means any way of sharing money among more people.

revenue

Revenue is the money that a company or person receives from making or doing things.

royalties

Royalties are payments made to the copyright owner of a work whenever it is sold.

software

Software is the program or instructions that tell a computer what to do.

stock

A stock is a certificate of ownership in a corporation.

stock market

A stock market can mean the same as a stock exchange—a place where stocks and shares are bought and sold.

tax

Tax is the money paid by people and companies to the government to help fund the running of the country.

tax haven

A tax haven is a place or country where taxes on incomes and wealth are either reduced or do not exist.

unemployment

Unemployment is when people do not have jobs.

usury

Usury is another name for charging interest on loans, especially at very high rates

World Bank

The World Bank is an international bank that lends money to countries for development.

Want to Learn More?

At the Library

Harman, Hollis Page. *Money Sense for Kids!* 2nd ed. Hauppauge, N.Y.: Barron's, 2004.

Karlitz, Gail. *Growing Money: A Complete Investing Guide for Kids.* New York: Price Stern Sloan, 1999.

Mayr, Diane. *The Everything Kids' Money Book: From Spending to Saving to Investing—Learn All About Money!* Holbrook, Mass.: Adams Media Corp., 2000.

Nathan, Amy. *The Kids' Allowance Book.* New York: Walker and Company, 1998.

Look for all the books in this series:

Common Cents
The Money in Your Pocket
0-7565-1671-4

Cowries, Coins, Credit
The History of Money
0-7565-1676-5

Get Rich Quick?
Earning Money
0-7565-1674-9

Money: It's Our Job
Money Careers
0-7565-1675-7

Save, Spend, Share
Using Your Money
0-7565-1672-2

What's It All Worth?
The Value of Money
0-7565-1673-0

On the Web

For more information on *the value of money*, use FactHound to track down Web sites related to this book.

1. Go to *www.facthound.com*
2. Type in a search word related to this book or this book ID: 0756516730
3. Click on the *Fetch It* button.
Your trusty FactHound will fetch the best Web sites for you!

Index